A Spark Of Inspiration

Edited By Allanah Jackson-James

First published in Great Britain in 2020 by:

Young Writers
Remus House
Coltsfoot Drive
Peterborough
PE2 9BF
Telephone: 01733 890066
Website: www.youngwriters.co.uk

Printed and bound in the UK by BookPrintingUK
Website: www.bookprintinguk.com
YB0442A

FOREWORD

Here at Young Writers our defining aim is to promote the joys of reading and writing to children and young adults and we are committed to nurturing the creative talents of the next generation. By allowing them to see their own work in print we believe their confidence and love of creative writing will grow.

Out Of This World is our latest fantastic competition, specifically designed to encourage the writing skills of primary school children through the medium of poetry. From the high quality of entries received, it is clear that it really captured the imagination of all involved.

We are proud to present the resulting collection of poems that we are sure will amuse and inspire.

An absorbing insight into the imagination and thoughts of the young, we hope you will agree that this fantastic anthology is one to delight the whole family again and again.

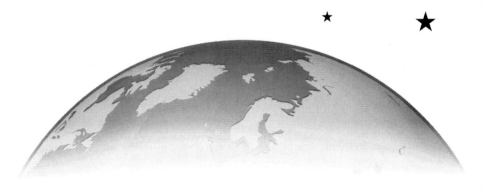

CONTENTS

Esmee Davis (9)	63
Oscar Brunton (9)	64
Ethan Todd (8)	65
Abigail Gardner (9)	66

Fairfields Primary School & Nursery, Flamstead End

Kayleigh Hickman (9)	67
Henry Brillus (9)	68
Alex Wersocki (8)	70
Sophia Mackenzie (8)	72
Jamie Joyce (8)	74
Ethan Wotton (8)	76
Sonny Bullock (8)	78
Lily Goodridge (9)	79
Ryker Wilcox (9)	80
Sophianna Louca (9)	81
Phoebe Rose Jennings (8)	82
Rafe Allen (8)	83
Rochelle Jayomanne (9)	84
Josh Russell (8)	85
Ollie Clowes (9)	86
Sophia Panahori (9)	87
Hope Simmons (9)	88
Molly Hemmett (8)	89
Elisa Ovayolu (8)	90
Christian Mouskoudi (8)	91
Bobby Cornwell (9)	92
Aaron Lessells (9)	93
Isabella Gibson (9)	94
Amy Rose Powell (9)	95
Shanai Brown (9)	96
Ishan Khan (8)	97
Rosey Paddick (8)	98
Luke Achilleos (9)	99
Isla Davis (8)	100
Kaelan Marsh (8)	101
Abigail Needs (9)	102
Sienna Conway (8)	103
Freddie Woods (8)	104
Thomas Jaselsky (9)	105
Oliver Noble (9)	106
Charlotte Collie (8)	107

Estelle Sodeke-Guerra (8)	108
Quinlan Riley (5)	109
Theo Achilleos (9)	110
Ethan Thomas (8)	111
Ella Carroll (8)	112
Millie-Lee Dwyer (8)	113
Amira Bundu (8)	114
Fearne James (9)	115
Aksel Acemgil (8)	116

Piper Hill High School, Newall Green

Raamin Islam (14)	117
Adam Alferjani (12)	118
Harry Norman Archebald (16)	119
Salim Alqahtani (14)	120
Tamzin Eyles (14)	121
Freya Wilkinson (13)	122
Tia Deal (12)	123
Max Gandy (15)	124
Bennett Tomy (14)	125
Georgina Johnson (15)	126
Leo Senobari (12)	127
Ryan Johnson (13)	128

Southborough Primary School, Bromley

Rachael Smith (8)	129
Lauren Bewsey (8)	130
Finley Johnston (8)	132
Emma-Louisa Marie Minas (8)	133
Rhea Chowdhury (8)	134
Jessica Wallace (9)	135
Lacey Hodson (8)	136
Jake Wigley (9)	137
Daniel Cooke (9)	138
Benjamin Redgrave (8)	139
Oliver Jack Dobbs (9)	140
Archie Beaumont (8)	141
Melisa Bafli (9)	142
Billy Cranenburgh (8)	143

Southmuir Primary School, Kirriemuir

Maia Valentine (11)	144
Daniel Buist (12)	145
Kieron Robertson (9)	146
Caitlyn Fraser (11)	147
Keirra Brough (11)	148
Ross Brown (10)	149
Oscar Gray (11)	150
Rose Pyott (11)	151
Liam Mcintosh (10)	152
Thomas Watson (11)	153
Cameron Kelman (11)	154
Caela Wallace (11)	155
Murray Small (10)	156
Tia Munro (11)	157

St Raphael's Catholic Primary School, Stalybridge

Oliver Richardson (10)	158
Bethany Gibbons (9)	160
Katie Wright-Borges (9)	161
Poppy Evans	162
Harvey Wade (9)	163
Wiktoria Weglarek (10)	164
Hunter Melville-Terry (9)	165
Sophie Hunt (9)	166
Bethan Hillier (9)	167
Thomas Rothwell (10)	168
Oscar Newton (9)	170
Matilda Costello (9)	171
Jesse Kyeyune (9)	172
Tremaine Norton (10)	173
Riley Norton (9)	174
Kian Cassin (10)	175
Alice Jones (9)	176
Thomas Barrientos (9)	177
James Bardsley (9)	178
Katie Cooke (9)	179
Frankie Dutton (10)	180
Archie Blay (9)	181
Belle Forrest (10)	182

Keira Lee (9)	183

St Stephen's CE (VA) Primary School, Burnley

Richard Mankovecky (9)	184
Joshua Wooding (9)	185
Ophelia Sedgwick (9)	186
Miley Milliken (10)	187
Nicole Lord (9)	188
Hollie Murdoch (10) & Amelia Little-Peddar (9)	189
Harry Morton-Hargreaves (9)	190
Amelia Parsons (10)	191
Markus Mankovecky (9)	192
Georgina Pilling (10)	193
Dexter Bennett-Hope (9)	194
Jovi Fifield (10)	195
Harun Mitchell-Celep (9)	196
Lucca Murgatroyd (9)	197
Paris Hewitt (10)	198

THE POEMS

Moon Is Shining!

This evening he got up,
On the grumpy side of the bed,
Shut the blue space curtains,
And leant his head,
Back out of the grey window.
His bright laziness,
Spilling over,
Scattering shadows in every way.
Plunging the world into greyness.
Giving more bore,
To the back of the sun,
And blackening all the world.
Then without any warning,
As if he was suddenly bored,
Or just sulky,
Because no one was awake,
Giving praise
To his shimmering ways.
Moon closed the sky window,
With a thundering boom,
Plunging the whole wide world in to doom.

Mya Gleeson (9)
Brackley CE Junior School, Brackley

1

Afternoon Comes

Afternoon comes,
With a small football kicking.

Afternoon comes,
With the little babies feeding.

Afternoon comes,
With controller batteries going.

Afternoon comes,
With brother shouting.

Afternoon comes,
With glass shattering.

Afternoon comes,
With parents' very loud banging.

Afternoon comes,
With sister snatching.

Afternoon comes,
With feet stomping.

Afternoon comes,
With me gaming.

Afternoon comes,
With the moon turning on.

Oliver Davies (9)
Brackley CE Junior School, Brackley

Space Soup

Take...
A splash of colour,
A huge black hole
That sucks you in,
A humongous white glowing moon.

Add plenty of yellow shapes,
The black sky
A star painting,
(With a long trail),
A big orange fading
Into a yellow ball.

The yellow shapes
Talking to each other.
The brown ball
Flying like Superman,
People floating around,
Eight planets and one dwarf planet.

Now just keep everything you have,
Anytime,

Then all you have to do
Is wait.

Kyla Martin (9)

Brackley CE Junior School, Brackley

Pokémon Soup

Take
A cat Pokémon.
Let him scratch,
Find him an enemy.
Has he met his match?

Add a worm Pokémon,
Let him eat the liver.
He looks like a caterpillar,
He makes you shiver.

Mix them in a bowl,
Add fire and ice.
Then put them in the oven,
Because they taste nice!

The Pokémon is a cool creature of wonder,
Its hands were furry like they were wearing gloves.
A measly Pokémon is your best friend,
Some Pokémon are red doves.

Hayden Lehec (8)
Brackley CE Junior School, Brackley

Meteors Are Not...

Meteors are not
Round, jagged, hard rocks
Smashed by the infuriated
Immortal gods in anger.
Neither are they
Soft, white snowballs, being flung
Carelessly by joyful children.
They're not even
The heavy metal cannonballs
Being shot out with extreme force
By dangerous, hard cannons.
They aren't
A pumped-up, pattered football,
Being kicked super hard
Across a field by an enranged footballer.
Never is it
Microscopic light white snow
Being sprinkled everywhere.

Kaidyn Kong (9)
Brackley CE Junior School, Brackley

Evening Comes

Evening comes,
With nice Mum cooking.

Evening comes,
With the blue front door closing.

Evening comes,
With shiny plates clanging.

Evening comes,
With kind dog barking.

Evening comes,
With me and lovely brother playing.

Evening comes,
With nice Mum shouting.

Evening comes,
With family chomping.

Evening comes,
With knife and forking dinging.

Evening comes,
To turn off the sun,
Time to sleep.

Sophie Hounslow (8)

Brackley CE Junior School, Brackley

School Comes With...

School comes,
With lovely teachers teaching.

School comes,
With curious children learning.

School comes,
With joyful children playing.

School comes,
With the loud bell ringing.

School comes,
With beautiful teachers clapping.

School comes,
With lovely children singing.

School comes,
With playful children eating.

School comes,
With the end-of-the-day prayer,
With the bright red door opening.

Ruby Twomey (9)
Brackley CE Junior School, Brackley

Evening Comes

Evening comes,
Bedtime!
With me cheekily delaying.

Evening comes,
With my little brother crying.

Evening comes,
With parents saying,
"Dinner time, darling!"

Evening comes,
With me and my little sister laughing.

Evening comes,
With me nicely bathing.

Evening comes,
With me loudly snoring.

Evening comes,
To drag me into bed -
Time to turn off everything.
Goodnight!

Matilda Campbell (8)
Brackley CE Junior School, Brackley

Lunchtime Comes

Lunchtime comes,
With noisy children chomping.
Lunchtime comes,
With big lunch boxes banging.
Lunchtime comes,
With energised children running.
Lunchtime comes,
With awesome teachers clapping.
Lunchtime comes,
With crazy people talking.
Lunchtime comes,
With bored children groaning.
Lunchtime comes,
With talkative teachers talking.
Lunchtime comes,
To drag me into the room
Of noisiness
And to make me feel blue.

Florence Taylor-Muff (9)
Brackley CE Junior School, Brackley

Pets Come With...

Pets come,
With big dogs woofing.
Pets come,
With fluffy cats sleeping.
Pets come,
With vicious snakes hissing.
Pets come,
With little birds singing.
Pets come,
With hairy tarantulas moving.
Pets come,
With colourful parrots talking.
Pets come,
With hyper lizards crunching.
Pets come,
With guinea pigs nibbling.
Pets come,
With Royal Mail ripping.
Pets come,
To give me chores -
A tired morning.

Scarlett Cook (9)
Brackley CE Junior School, Brackley

The Super Sun

The sun is not
A fireball getting booted
Up high in the sky.

Neither is it
A squishy, warm meatball
Flicked up in the air
With delicious bolognese.

It is not even
An orange paintball
That you can't see how fast it goes
Shot up in the sky.

It isn't
A tiny, fast, gold coin
Spinning in the air.

Never is it
Like a lightbulb
Switching on and off
For night and day.

Louis Youens (8)
Brackley CE Junior School, Brackley

Lunchtime Comes With...

Lunchtime comes,
With shining plates rattling.

Lunchtime comes,
With lovely food flying.

Lunchtime comes,
With children chatting.

Lunchtime comes,
With tummy rumbling.

Lunchtime comes,
With bell talking.

Lunchtime comes,
With squirrels climbing.

Lunchtime comes,
With classroom door closing.

Lunchtime comes,
To give us food
And make our bellies full.

Skye Gardner (9)
Brackley CE Junior School, Brackley

Dynamic Dogs

Dogs are not...
Olympic runners
Always getting gold medals
With neon green ribbon around it.

Neither are they...
Cuddly blankets
That sleep with you
Every night.

They're not even...
Alarm clocks
With tails
Woofing at the people going to the toilet next
door.

They aren't...
Great footballers
Winning every match,
With medals that are shaped
Like dog bones.

Erin Griffiths (9)
Brackley CE Junior School, Brackley

Night

Night comes,
With a loud dog barking.

Night comes,
With excited Mum screaming.

Night comes,
With small TV shouting.

Night comes,
With massive remote falling.

Night comes,
With tiny dog scratching.

Night comes,
With tired Dad snoring.

Night comes,
With me just always chilling.

Night comes,
With the moon shining
All of her light on us.

Caleb Thorne (9)
Brackley CE Junior School, Brackley

Evening Comes With...

Evening comes,
With shower running.

Evening comes,
With me reading.

Evening comes,
With annoying Alexa talking.

Evening comes,
With an exciting Switch.

Evening comes,
With big sister snitching.

Evening comes,
With me gaming.

Evening comes,
With lights flickering.

Evening comes,
With God turning the sun down
And getting into bed.

Deven Fothergill (8)
Brackley CE Junior School, Brackley

Epic Earth

The Earth is like a blue marble,
But some of its gases are harmful.
The Earth has brilliant people
That can think,
Let's hope they don't go extinct!

The atmosphere has gases,
That you'll learn in science classes,
Like nitrogen and oxygen.

Animals stampede,
Over the fields,
To get their meals.

Climate change is really bad,
So let's help,
The glorious land.

Leon Keirl (8)
Brackley CE Junior School, Brackley

Night-Time

Night-time comes,
With stairs creaking.
Night-time comes,
With toothbrush scrubbing.
Night-time comes,
With the wind blowing.
Night-time comes,
With the clock ticking.
Night-time comes,
With owls hooting.
Night-time comes,
With babies crying.
Night-time comes,
With people snoring.
Night-time comes,
With doors slamming.
Night-time comes,
With the grey light turning on.

Lily Goss (8)
Brackley CE Junior School, Brackley

Come Out, Moon

The moon is not...
A huge eye watching you,
Waiting to tell you what to do.

Neither is it...
Huge, curved, yellow bananas
At the top of the fruity sky.

It's not even...
A massive, greyish balloon
In the playground sky.

It's not...
A bright torch shining
On your house at night.

The moon is like...
A romantic candle in the sky,
On your honeymoon.

Kaitlin Hyde (9)
Brackley CE Junior School, Brackley

The Hot Sun

The sun is not
A blue netball being thrown around
By crazy children
Training for netball club.

Neither is it
A small orange flower
Swaying elegantly in the wind,
Like an audience swaying to a song.

It is not even
A disco ball
Partying all night long to a song.

It is not even
A heavy white golf ball in the breezy air
Aiming for a small hole in the crumbly earth.

Rosie Jones (8)
Brackley CE Junior School, Brackley

Galaxy Soup

Take,
A nip of the night,
A bucket of colours,
And a pinch of stardust.

Add the bottle of stars,
A sprinkle of shimmer
(Just for the sky),
A handful of glitter.

The sliver of beauty,
The bright shine of the moon,
The sprinkle of hearts,
With plenty of moonlight.

Now keep it quite warm,
And serve any time,
Then all you have to do,
Is wait!

Harriet Jones (9)
Brackley CE Junior School, Brackley

Movie Life

Haiku poetry

Batman doesn't like
Bad guys like Bane and Scarecrow
Batman will get them.

He is so awesome
He's like a cool assassin
He is Spider-Man.

Green Lantern was a
Pilot in the olden days
He has a green ring.

Superman is an
Alien sent to the Earth
Can shoot laser beams.

Harry Potter has
A brilliant friend who dies
By mean Voldemort.

Elliott Bush (9)
Brackley CE Junior School, Brackley

Super Cute Dogs

Dogs are not...
Crazy, playful, funny children
On a summer's afternoon.
Neither are they...
A warm, fluffy, comfortable pillow
That you lay your head on at night.
They're not even...
Like a white, glimmering, soft,
Sparkly unicorn,
With snow-white wings.
They're not even...
Strong, lightning-speed runners
In a race for a charity.

Casey Esterhiuzen (8)
Brackley CE Junior School, Brackley

Cute Fluffy Hamsters

Hamsters are not...
Adorable, fluffy teddies
That can move.

Neither are they
Fluffy balls
That eat all day long.

They are not even...
Handwarmers sleeping in the day,
Although they're really warm
And cuddly.

They aren't...
Really fluffy pom-poms.

They're not even...
Like a soft, fluffy carpet.

Alice Gray (9)
Brackley CE Junior School, Brackley

Sparkly Snow

Snow is not candyfloss
That good children love to eat
When they're nice.

Neither is it
Cotton wool that is soft
Like a cosy blanket you curl up in all day
When you're feeling under the weather.

It's not even
Fluffy paws that sit
On your lap all day.

They aren't
Ice cubes that give you brain freeze.

Marianna Konczak (9)
Brackley CE Junior School, Brackley

A Zooming Star

Planes are not,
A fast blur of pale paper,
Flapping like crazy.

Neither are they,
A flicker of a star,
Iceberg-white,
Blinding and tiny.

They're not even,
A chopped paper circle
Of chalk-white debris
Sleeping on
A Formula 1 circuit.

They aren't
A rip of a silvery-white card,
Like iron bars.

Oliver Nelson (8)
Brackley CE Junior School, Brackley

You Go, Dogs

Dogs are not...
Speedy marathon runners
Racing to the end
Of the doggie race.

Neither are they...
Fluffy blankets to snuggle with
On a freezing cold
Winter night.

They aren't...
Olympic swimmers
Trying to hold their breath.

They are...
As fluffy as a soft, cuddly,
Beautiful and sparkly cushion.

Holly Evans (9)
Brackley CE Junior School, Brackley

Football

Football comes,
With a whistle blowing.

Football comes,
With players kicking.

Football comes,
With the net dangling.

Football comes,
With grass whooshing.

Football comes,
With people talking.

Football comes,
With people shouting.

Football comes,
With a goal saved.

Jacob (8)
Brackley CE Junior School, Brackley

What Planets Are

Planets are not,
Massive colourful footballs,
In the solar system,
Floating about.

Neither are they,
Gigantic meteors,
Shooting across in the air.

They're not even,
The enormous stars of entertainment.
No.

Planets are planets,
Planets are the orbs of life and
Big rocks of defence.

Jeziel Lopes (8)
Brackley CE Junior School, Brackley

What Planets Are

Planets are not,
Massive footballs,
Floating about.

Neither are they,
Gigantic stars,
Spinning in the solar system.

They're not even,
Huge meteors,
Orbiting the sun.

No.
Planets are planets.
The orbs of life.
They're like massive pieces of rock,
Water, dust and stones.

Heyden Watton (9)
Brackley CE Junior School, Brackley

Sunrise, Morning

Sunrise comes,
With the room warming, brightening.
Sunrise comes,
With the shower running.
Sunrise comes,
With coffee beans grinding.
Sunrise comes,
With my dad still snoring.
Sunrise comes,
With alarm clocks ringing.
Sunrise comes,
With me tossing and turning.
Sunrise comes,
With me, eating.

Billy Allen (8)
Brackley CE Junior School, Brackley

Evening

Evening comes,
With lovely Mum cooking.
Evening comes,
With frying pan fizzing.
Evening comes,
With sofa sitting.
Evening comes,
With high-pitched screaming.
Evening comes,
With TV flashing.
Evening comes,
With fast Nerf guns shooting.
Evening comes,
To drag me into bed.
Lights out.

Scott Pickford (8)
Brackley CE Junior School, Brackley

Beautiful Ketchup

Ketchup is not
Someone's slippery, slimy blood
Falling down like a waterfall.

Neither is it
A beautiful heart
Keeping your body alive.

It is not even
A massive, colourful,
Bright red card.

It isn't
A shiny clean cup.
It's definitely not
A blinding red light.

Harrison Cosby (8)
Brackley CE Junior School, Brackley

What Time Is

Time is not
The battery
That powers the sun.

Neither is it
A thing you depend on
To get you through your day.

It's not even
The referee
For the sun and moon.

No.
Time is time,
The constant track
That lets us know
What's happening
In our lives.

Tom Prinsep (8)
Brackley CE Junior School, Brackley

Diva Dolphins

Dolphins are not...
Crescent moons
Jumping out of the glimmering,
Dark blue sea,
With the beautiful silver moon
Shining on it.

Neither are they
Rubber bath toys
Squirting water
Like a whale.

They aren't even...
A purpley-blue flower
Floating in the glittery ocean.

Erin Elsworth (8)
Brackley CE Junior School, Brackley

The Hot Sun

The sun is not
Like a flying meatball
In a sky of spaghetti.

Neither is it
A yellow pom-pom,
Nice and fluffy.

It is
A laser
Too hot to handle.

It isn't
A big yellow disco
In the baby blue sky.

The sun is
As bright as a shiny coin.

Maisy (8)
Brackley CE Junior School, Brackley

The Glimmering Sun

The sun is not
A yellow football being kicked in the sky.

Neither is it
A huge full stop on your best work.

It is not even
Cut up yellow paper
For a little boy's work.

It isn't
Tiny bits of sand
In a boy's garden.

Hugo Price (9)

Brackley CE Junior School, Brackley

The Bright Sun

The sun is not
Like a ginormous meatball
On a huge sky-blue plate.

Neither is it
The yellow pom-pom of the universe.

It is not even
A gigantic fireball
Gliding in the air.

It is not
A huge gold coin
Of the world.

Zac Norton (8)
Brackley CE Junior School, Brackley

Famous Places

London is busy.
Brackley is our home, yippee!
Brazil is so hot.

France won the World Cup,
So they are the best team
In the World Cup, woohoo!

Finland is a fridge,
Sledges all day,
Then go to get changed
To go to bed.

Jack Heather (8)
Brackley CE Junior School, Brackley

Scenic Sky

The sky is scenic,
Floating unbreakable sky,
High up.
Up and away.

Clouds are lovely,
Floating pillows in the sky.
Can I have a nap?

Rain, boring rain,
I hate it.
It's the worst,
It leaves puddles.

Thomas Lawson (8)
Brackley CE Junior School, Brackley

Chinese Dragon

Haiku poetry

Orange crystal eyes,
Horrible, pale, deadly scales.
Chinese dragon, cool.

You could hate a burn,
Fire as bright as the sun, wow.
Don't go to China.

It is a tiger,
It is a lion, uh-oh.
Chinese dragon, what?

Elleanor Hine (8)
Brackley CE Junior School, Brackley

The Shiny Sun

The burning hot sun,
A face spying through the clouds,
A bowl in the sky.

A clock in the sky,
The disco lights in the sky,
A scrunchie up high.

An orange flower,
A gold coin in the blue sky,
A giant meatball.

Elise Rayner (8)
Brackley CE Junior School, Brackley

The Sparkling Boiling Hot Sun

The glimmering hot sun,
The sun makes every house hot,
The sun is boiling.

The cotton wool sun,
Ovens are hot like the sun,
The sun is hot too.

The sun is awesome,
The sun is boiling hot,
The sun is burning.

Amber Buxey (8)
Brackley CE Junior School, Brackley

The Sun

Haiku poetry

The sun is shining,
It is a glittery ball.
It's hot like fire.

It is powerful,
Like a lightbulb in the sky,
It is bright like gold.

The sun is lava,
Above the clouds, the sun sits,
Warming the world up.

Mia Jones (8) & Joe Spittle (9)
Brackley CE Junior School, Brackley

Scrummy Sandwiches

Yummy ham in bread,
Yellow cheese in a bun,
Fishy tuna. Yum!

Like the large, red sun,
A flaming red tomato,
Scrumptious salad, yum!

Fishy tuna, wow!
Delicious egg and cheese, yum!
Scrumptious salad, what?

Lucy Potter (8)
Brackley CE Junior School, Brackley

Around The World

Haiku poetry

London like a jam
Might need a taxi to get
Around to places

England is so cool
Where we like to go to school
We love England lots

Portugal has lots
Of lovely beaches where you
Go and have a splash.

Oliver Moulder (8)
Brackley CE Junior School, Brackley

The Sun

The sun is a ball,
Glittering over the world,
Like a juicy orange.
Like a boiling rock,
Sitting on the universe,
Like a fireball.
Bright like a big light,
Glittering ball of fire,
The big light is bright.

Matthew Du Plooy (8) & Lloyd Kuhn (9)

Brackley CE Junior School, Brackley

Candyfloss Is Not

Candyfloss is not,
A yummy cloud in the sky,
A soft sheep getting sheared,
A pom-pom on your nice boots,
Wool on your silver carpet,
A piece of fluff under your couch.

Jacob Williams (9)
Brackley CE Junior School, Brackley

Night-Time

Night-time comes,
With loud stairs creaking.
Night-time comes,
With toothbrush scrubbing.
Night-time comes,
With the wind howling.
Night-time comes.

Imogen Gargan (8)
Brackley CE Junior School, Brackley

Football

Football comes,
With whistle blowing.

Football comes,
With goal saving.

Football comes,
With players passing.

Charlie Canning (8)

Brackley CE Junior School, Brackley

Blue Dolphins

Dolphins are not,
The king of the sea
And of sea creatures,
The king of the whales,
Pointy knives,
Giant whales.

Max Finch (8)
Brackley CE Junior School, Brackley

The Super Dog

A haiku

Dogs run like lightning,
Dogs bark like a car engine,
Dogs are a fluff ball.

Riley Borton (9)
Brackley CE Junior School, Brackley

Mars

Mars is as orange as orange peel,
Mars is as circular as a football,
Mars tastes like cheese,
Mars lives in space,
Mars smells like sand,
Mars sounds like wind.

Antonina Renata Wojciechowska (10)
Corran Integrated Primary School, Larne

All About Dogs

D ogs diving in the fresh river.
O n and on they go.
G oing faster every time.
S plashing water.

S wimming with their friends.
W inning races to the ball.
I n the water, they jump.
M agic fresh water.
M ysterious water splashes.
I n the water, they learn to swim.
N ever stop having fun.
G etting better every day.

Grace Nolan (8)
Crossley Street Primary School, Wetherby

The Seaside

S plashing waves crashing against the black, ragged rocks.

E veryone's chatting like a noisy zoo.

A mazing blue, clear, glittering sea.

S eagulls chirping like mad everywhere.

I n the noisy arcade, coins clatter in the two-pence machines.

D iving off the high, black, steep rocks into the splashing waves.

E veryone's children making sandcastles everywhere.

Ellisia Anderson (9)

Crossley Street Primary School, Wetherby

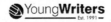
Kids Swimming

K ids have fun in the sea.
I t's a crystal-blue sea.
D eep blue sea to swim in.

S easpray covering kids' faces.
W ater splashing and making waves.
I surf on waves.
M aking a mark on the rock.
M arks covering rocks.
I can smell fish and chips.
N ight-blue ocean.
G iant big blue waves.

Abigail Williams (8)
Crossley Street Primary School, Wetherby

Fossils

F ossils can be any size, no matter how small.

O minous feelings fill my crazy head.

S alty water surrounds me like air.

S eek out, that's what I should do.

I mmense fossil this is, I wonder what happened?

L ost at sea I must be. Where am I?

S harks are probably watching me, what should I do?

Aidan Mooney (9)
Crossley Street Primary School, Wetherby

Sea Floor

Treasure scattered amongst the frightening sharks,
Little fish hiding in gaps everywhere inside the
rough rocks,
Colourful coral spread out on the sea floor,
A rotten ship stands covered in green fungus,
The dark ocean bed seems a long way down,
Rainbowfish swimming past to crazy depths,
All is quiet but what could be lurking below?

Ethan King (8)
Crossley Street Primary School, Wetherby

Sea Life

Speedy swimming,
Fish gleaming,
Sharks hunting,
Coral glowing,
Sea snakes slithering,
Clownfish laughing,
Octopuses inking,
I start sinking,
Blue whales rising,
Goldfish shimmering,
Shipwreck treasure gleaming,
I rise to the surface to take a breath.
I love the sea.

Sebastian Davis (9)
Crossley Street Primary School, Wetherby

Crashing Waves

I can see wavy waves crashing
Towards colossal, ragged rocks.
I can feel the water
Bashing against my sunburn.
I can hear jet skis speeding
Across the crystal-blue sea.
I can smell
Delicious fish and chips.
I can hear the music playing
While the coins clatter
In the arcade.

Max Barrett (8)
Crossley Street Primary School, Wetherby

At The Olympics

O lympics only.

L ook at me, awaiting victory!

Y es, take your marks - go!

M y destiny awaits.

P rofessional swimmer with every stroke.

I n a world of my own, I win.

C an I do it?

S peeding to the finish line.

Esmee Davis (9)

Crossley Street Primary School, Wetherby

Deep-Sea Divers

S norkelling swimmers.
W ater as clear as glass.
I t is as clear as crystal.
M ysterious deep-sea creatures.
M aking bubbles.
I cy-cold water.
N early bitten by a shark.
G reen coral.

Oscar Brunton (9)
Crossley Street Primary School, Wetherby

Swimming

S ea waving in the wind.

W ater very clear.

I t's as clear as crystals.

M ysterious creatures.

M agical fish.

I t is fantastic.

N ewfound fish.

G igantic shark.

Ethan Todd (8)

Crossley Street Primary School, Wetherby

Waves

A haiku

Waves are colossal
They crash against jagged rocks
Ripples are gorgeous.

Abigail Gardner (9)

Crossley Street Primary School, Wetherby

A Magical Display

A rtistic work in the sky.

M onkeys there, whizzing by.

A ngels fly and light up the night.

G orgeous, colourful and bright.

I cy colours, rainbow colours, all are the best.

C olours, colours, splendid colours. What about the rest?

A ny colours, I really don't mind.

L ike them all, even if I'm blind.

D on't get hurt!

I know you can touch some dirt (but don't).

S o, go and have fun.

P lay and watch till they're done.

L ime green, yellow and blue.

A n act of colour, just for you.

Y oung or old, have some fun. Watch till they're done.

Kayleigh Hickman (9)
Fairfields Primary School & Nursery, Flamstead End

Fireworks

Fireworks, fireworks,
Shine so bright.
Fireworks, fireworks,
Light so bright.

They fizzle, they crack,
They burst open wide.
They crackle, they bang,
They make a big fright.

Fireworks, fireworks,
Light up the sky.
Fireworks, fireworks,
In the sky they fly.

They whizz, they shrivel,
They let out a shower.
The pop, they burn,
They bang with their power.

Fireworks, fireworks,
Are so amazing.

Fireworks, fireworks,
They'll get you gazing.
They fizzle, they crackle,
They're all over the place.
They crack, they bang
At a pace.

Fireworks, fireworks,
Light up the dark.
Fireworks, fireworks,
Making a mark.
They crackle, they bang,
In there, they blast.
They fizzle, they pop,
They've gone at last.

Henry Brillus (9)
Fairfields Primary School & Nursery, Flamstead End

2020

Fireworks, fireworks,
Sizzling in the sky.
The noise they make
Is giving me a fright.
Fireworks, fireworks,
Flying so high,
Smiling through my window inside.

In the sky,
I see an explosion.
Inside the firework
There's a potion.
The fireworks are racing
And I think it's amazing.

Fireworks, fireworks,
Silent and loud,
In one firework,
There's a lot of sounds.
Fireworks, fireworks,
Loud with heat inside.

Soon I'm gonna meet my friends
On a loud night.

Crackle, boom!
Crackle, boom!
Up, up
And away!

Fireworks, fireworks,
Placed with care.
It's 2020,
Our poem ends there.

Alex Wersocki (8)
Fairfields Primary School & Nursery, Flamstead End

Fireworks

Fireworks, fireworks,
Popping in the sky.
Crackle, sparkle, whizzing
As they go by.

Fireworks, fireworks,
Extremely fast.
Glowing and beautiful,
I wonder how long they will last.

Fireworks, fireworks,
Banging and bright.
Colourful and rainbow,
They will last all night.

Fireworks, fireworks,
Glittering and pink.
Purple and loud,
It makes me wink.

Fireworks, fireworks,
Coral and white.

Exploding so loudly,
It gives me a fright.

Fireworks, fireworks,
Fizzing in the air.
Multicoloured and blue,
Fizzing everywhere.

Sophia Mackenzie (8)

Fairfields Primary School & Nursery, Flamstead End

Fireworks

Fireworks are bright,
And fireworks are light.
Whizz! Bang! Pop!
Fast as a cheetah,
Pop! Stop!
With a swirl, with a twirl,
Frazzle!
With a bang!
The fireworks separate to the moon.

Fireworks, fireworks,
Fireworks sizzling away!
Really loud,
Making me so high up,
To the sky!
Sparkly light,
Going up a pipe,
Fireworks flying,
Up to my room.

Coming as fast as a lion,
Really warm,

Coming to a storm of fireworks!
Fireworks!
Fireworks rule,
Fireworks are cool,
And I sit on a stool.

Jamie Joyce (8)
Fairfields Primary School & Nursery, Flamstead End

Fireworks

Fireworks, fireworks,
Amazing and hot.
Fireworks, fireworks,
Make you go, "What?!"
Fireworks, fireworks,
Wonderful and flabbergasting.
Fireworks, fireworks,
All they do is blasting.

Fireworks bright,
Fireworks have height.
Fireworks crackle and zoom,
Fireworks crackle and boom.

Fireworks, fireworks,
Hurt my eyes.
Fireworks, fireworks,
Every time my sister cries.

Fireworks fizzing.
Fireworks buzzing.

Fireworks grasping.
Fireworks gasping.

The fireworks went off for 2020!

Ethan Wotton (8)
Fairfields Primary School & Nursery, Flamstead End

Fireworks

Fireworks, fireworks,
Gleaming everywhere,
Colours bursting everywhere.
Bang!
Fireworks explode,
With a smash of gold,
And the people shiver with cold!

Fireworks fizzle
And crackle like popcorn.
Fireworks are bright
And they have a good flight,
Sparkling, popping out crimson.
The kids watch 'The Simpsons'.

Fireworks explode,
With a little pop of joy.
Fireworks are bright
And always give a fright!
They're red and made of sparkles
And always are there to crackle.

Sonny Bullock (8)
Fairfields Primary School & Nursery, Flamstead End

A Magical Night

A lways so bright in the midnight sky!

M onkey shouting and leaping high!
A ngel's colours explode with fright!
G orgeous stars, all so big and flowery!
I magine you're in your own world.
C all all the people to see them.
A ll fireworks are making people clap and cheer.
L ily pads are leaping like

N ever before.
I n a cave where they explode.
G azing in like the amazing
H orizon sun.
T onight is where our hearts lead us!

Lily Goodridge (9)
Fairfields Primary School & Nursery, Flamstead End

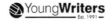
Whirling Magic

At night when the fireworks glow,
They feel like it's so slow,
The sparkle in the air in the dark,
It only gives you a little bit of spark.
When it's raining, all damp and cold,
Don't worry as you will see some gold.
While they're twirling,
You are whirling.
The fireworks don't stop there,
We think these fireworks are very rare.
So come down to the firework town,
Don't worry, we won't let you down.
What a shame,
The fireworks have gone away.
But don't worry,
Come again!

Ryker Wilcox (9)
Fairfields Primary School & Nursery, Flamstead End

Fireworks

F ireworks big and bright, see them zooming across your sky.

I n the night, sparkly fireworks appear before your eyes.

R un away from the blazing fireworks booming with loudness.

E xcellent fireworks fill the air with dazzling colours.

W hirling and twirling through the air.

O n the way home, bursting fireworks swallow the air.

R ainbows, rainbows in the night. Beautiful fizzing fireworks are bright.

K indness fills the air and fireworks too.

S o silent now, they are gone.

Sophianna Louca (9)

Fairfields Primary School & Nursery, Flamstead End

Fireworks Night

It's Fireworks Night,
The light shines bright.
Pop, crackle, bang.
The fireworks are up so high
Just like a mountain in the sky.
As you watch the colours shine,
Like the stars in the sky,
It's like glitter popping
In front of your eyes.

It sure is such a nice night
To be here tonight,
Such pretty colours,
Pink, green, blue,
Mum, where's the glue?
I want to make a firework too!
It's time to say goodnight,
To the firework's light.

Phoebe Rose Jennings (8)
Fairfields Primary School & Nursery, Flamstead End

Fireworks

F ireworks flying as high as a kite, booming as loud as a grenade.

I t's like a rainbow in the night sky or in the sunlight.

R eaching the moon and hearing fourteen colours about to bang.

E veryone here to see the fireworks and the bang.

W *hizz! Pop! Fizz! Zoom! Crackle!*

O ne night, fireworks exploded into light.

R umbling in the sky.

K eenly camping all night to listen to the fireworks.

Rafe Allen (8)

Fairfields Primary School & Nursery, Flamstead End

Pop!

Zap, zoom,
As I hear the fireworks boom.
Miracles happen to pop in the sky,
And it happens very, very high.

As everyone's faces glow,
The fireworks start to show,
As it zaps,
Everyone claps.

It's so colourful,
Oh my, why is it so wonderful?
As it's so breathtaking,
Why don't they just keep on making?

Oh fireworks, fireworks,
As everyone tries to work.

Rochelle Jayomanne (9)
Fairfields Primary School & Nursery, Flamstead End

Fireworks

F ireworks, fireworks, big and loud.

I gnite in the sky that makes them so high.

R ainbow colours flying into the sky.

E normous showers pouring down on me.

W onderful colours we all may see.

O ccasional sparklers, full of light.

R ed, orange, yellow, the crackling firework goes *bang!*

K *aboom!* goes the firework.

S ummersault they go, into thin air.

Josh Russell (8)
Fairfields Primary School & Nursery, Flamstead End

Fireworks, Fireworks

Fireworks, fireworks, banging in the sky,
As colourful as a rainbow,
Bang! Bang! Going sky-high,
Fireworks in my eyes, making them glow.

Fireworks, fireworks, as big as a tree,
In the crisp, cold air,
When fireworks are set off free,
Everybody comes off their chair.

The fireworks go fizz,
They go up in a flash,
The fireworks are sounding like a whizz,
When the colours clash.

Ollie Clowes (9)
Fairfields Primary School & Nursery, Flamstead End

Fireworks

Fireworks, fireworks,
Dazzling in the night.
Boom, crackle, fizzle,
Colourful, dangerous,
Beautiful and bright.
Fireworks, fireworks,
What a delight to see.
Pop, bang, whizz.

Fireworks, fireworks,
Dazzling in the night.
Fireworks, fireworks,
Dazzling with delight.
Fireworks, fireworks,
I am flabbergasted.
Fireworks, fireworks,
All of them blasted.

Sophia Panahori (9)
Fairfields Primary School & Nursery, Flamstead End

Whizzing Fireworks

Fireworks whizzing around,
Turning yellow to blue,
The audience is going wow,
And they're going *boom!*

Everyone is getting hot chocolate,
So cosy and warm,
They're going as loud as a disco,
Thumping like an elephant,
Going *boom! Pow!*
Bang! Pop!

You can find magic
Wherever you look.
Sit back and relax,
All you need is a *boom!*

Hope Simmons (9)
Fairfields Primary School & Nursery, Flamstead End

Popping Rockets

Sparks shimmer in the sky,
So bright and light,
Like popping rockets in the sky.
They are as fast as anything.
I could fly.

I run so fast.
I could go so high.
I jump to the pump,
To fly it off to the sky.

But suddenly,
The audience goes.
But fireworks flow.
The audience turns back
And so do the fireworks.
They become great friends
And that's the end.

Molly Hemmett (8)
Fairfields Primary School & Nursery, Flamstead End

Rainbow Firework

Fireworks all about
Rainbows in the sky.
I love fireworks with all my heart.
When they go up they say bye,
I see it with all of its heat.

Zooming up in colours,
Dark and light fire in the sky.
Some are slower,
The fireworks go in the sky,
So high.

I run to see fireworks,
Standing behind the fence and see,
The fireworks always work,
I always scream.

Elisa Ovayolu (8)
Fairfields Primary School & Nursery, Flamstead End

Fireworks Bang!

F ireworks are loud and bright.

I saw a firework display.

R avishing red was the first one.

E verybody had to run to see them.

W hizzing in the sky, the fireworks went by.

O range was another one, a bright colour like the sky.

R ed is a lovely colour too.

K *aboom!* went the fireworks.

S ometimes scary but oh so pretty.

Christian Mouskoudi (8)

Fairfields Primary School & Nursery, Flamstead End

Poppers

Zap, zoom,
Here they come.
They're flying high,
They go bang,
So many times.
Different colours,
Flying so high.
Some are big
And some are small.

They fly higher than the trees,
They go pop!
They go bang!
People go, "Oooh!"
People go, "Ahhh!"
It's the best.
People say,
"That was amazing!"

Bobby Cornwell (9)
Fairfields Primary School & Nursery, Flamstead End

Fireworks Dazzle!

Fireworks, fireworks so bright.
Fizz, crackle, pop,
Such a dazzling delight.
They fall with such a slop.

Fireworks, fireworks,
A huge flame.
Bang, crackle, fizz,
So make sure you aim.
Clap, clap with a hiss.

Fireworks, fireworks so hot.
Fizzle, hiss, clap,
Make sure to clap a lot.
Before they go down with a slap.

Aaron Lessells (9)
Fairfields Primary School & Nursery, Flamstead End

Fireworks

Sparks and glitter everywhere,
Fizzing and whizzing in the air.
As colourful as a rainbow,
Exploding like a big volcano!

As loud as a party popper,
As scary as Harry Potter.
Shooting quickly in the air,
Gives everybody a big scare!

Sparkling with colours,
Crimson, pink and blue.
Dancing fireworks in the air,
Whilst everybody is standing there.

Isabella Gibson (9)
Fairfields Primary School & Nursery, Flamstead End

Crackle! Pop! Bang!

Firework, firework,
As the sun goes down,
Everyone seems sad.
I see people are sad,
They have a frown,
It's Fireworks Night.

It goes round and round,
It's so pretty,
As it goes bang, bang,
Is it in the ground?

Pink, green,
Red and blue,
I'm so sad,
I wish I could stay,
Bye-bye,
It was nice to see you.

Amy Rose Powell (9)
Fairfields Primary School & Nursery, Flamstead End

Hello To The Heavens Up High

There goes the one,
Up in the sky.
Say hello
To the heavens up high.

Oh, no,
Where did it go?
It was such a delight
To be here tonight.

It was the end of the night,
I didn't want to say goodnight,
Because it was such a big fright.

Then I went,
Oh no.
I wanted to stay,
Till the end of the night.

Shanai Brown (9)
Fairfields Primary School & Nursery, Flamstead End

New Year's Eve Fireworks

F ireworks.

I n the bright, starry, colourful sky.

R ockets shooting with colour.

E lectro, neon, every type of colour.

W *hizz, pop, bang,* exploding like a whirl of colours.

O n the ground to sky-high.

R unning, jumping, people excited.

K aleidoscope in the sky.

S afety first, though!

Ishan Khan (8)

Fairfields Primary School & Nursery, Flamstead End

Fireworks Pop!

Fireworks, fireworks,
Pop! Pop! Pop!
Fireworks, fireworks,
Hot! Hot! Hot!

Fireworks burst,
In the dark night,
Some go wrong,
And some go right.

Catherine wheels spin,
Dizzy, dizzy.
Some keep going,
Busy, busy.

Oh, I see fireworks in sight!
I love fireworks,
They're such a delight.

Rosey Paddick (8)
Fairfields Primary School & Nursery, Flamstead End

Rockets!

Rockets, rockets,
Pop so high,
When you see them,
Suddenly it's gone.
Oh, hello!
There's another one,
So bright in your eyes.

Catherine wheels,
Spinning so bright,
So fast, so fun,
You can't believe your eyes.

So amazing and hot,
Don't go near,
Or you'll burn your fingers.

Luke Achilleos (9)
Fairfields Primary School & Nursery, Flamstead End

Firework

F ireworks flying in the night.
I n the night sky, they explode with delight.
R ockets are flying with such joy.
E very boy and girl enjoy.
W inning the night with energy.
O h! Dear fireworks, please stay with me.
R ed, yellow, blue.
K *aboom! Crash! Bang! Whoo!*

Isla Davis (8)

Fairfields Primary School & Nursery, Flamstead End

Fireworks

Fireworks, fireworks,
Shooting up into the sky.

Sparkling rainbows
Shimmer with light.

Fireworks, fireworks,
Flying like dreams
Over people's heads.

Fireworks, fireworks,
Ping! Pang!
Bang! Shazam!

Such fantastic noises
Fill people with joy!

Kaelan Marsh (8)
Fairfields Primary School & Nursery, Flamstead End

Snap, Crackle And Pop

Snap, crackle and *pop.*
See them go up.
Wish, wash, whirl,
See them all swirl.

Red, orange and yellow,
Magical they all are.
Colourful, loud, bright,
Dazzling in the night.

Big, crazy
Fires are lit.
Fizz, whizz, bang,
Catherine wheels hang.

Abigail Needs (9)
Fairfields Primary School & Nursery, Flamstead End

Fireworks!

Crack! Bang! Snapple! Pop!
There goes the sound of the fireworks.
Mega, mighty rockets zooming over our heads.
Catherine wheels swirling like a ballerina.
Sparkles crackling like pop rocks.
Beautiful colours lighting up the night sky.
Pink, blue and purple dazzle up the world.
I love fireworks!

Sienna Conway (8)
Fairfields Primary School & Nursery, Flamstead End

Fireworks

F ireworks are beautiful.

I t's super bright.

R unning high in the sky.

E asy to watch.

W hizzing across the sky.

O h, so beautiful.

R ight, time for the big one!

K *aboom!*

S leeping with beautiful colours in dreams.

Freddie Woods (8)

Fairfields Primary School & Nursery, Flamstead End

Fireworks

Fireworks, fireworks,
So lovely and bright,
Really colourful
And really light.
They are so wonderful.

They're going lightning fast,
So boiling hot,
It really is a blast.
They're sometimes
As orange as a lynx.

They pop,
They bop,
They hop.

Thomas Jaselsky (9)
Fairfields Primary School & Nursery, Flamstead End

Fireworks

F ireworks go boom and pop.
I 'm watching colours explode so high.
R eally loud bangs with unique colours.
E ven when you're in bed.
W hatever I mean.
O n holiday or in your house.
R eally, I'm not lying.
K *aboom!*

Oliver Noble (9)

Fairfields Primary School & Nursery, Flamstead End

Fireworks, Fireworks

Fireworks, fireworks,
Oh so high,
Fireworks, fireworks,
In the sky.

Fireworks, fireworks,
Pow! and *crack!*
Fireworks, fireworks,
All the zaps.

Fireworks, fireworks,
Sadly goodbye,
Fireworks, fireworks,
Not in the sky.

Charlotte Collie (8)
Fairfields Primary School & Nursery, Flamstead End

Bang! Crackle! Pop!

Bang!
There goes another one,
Tumble above my tongue.

Crackle!
Glitter falls like raindrops.

Pop!
The crowd cheers,
People are in tears.

As people leave,
The fireworks are pleased.

What a lovely night.

Estelle Sodeke-Guerra (8)
Fairfields Primary School & Nursery, Flamstead End

Firework

Bang! goes the firework.
Three, two, one,
Goes the firework,
It blows up high,
With glory and rainbows flashing,
A crackle and fizz shoots up,
Like lightning.
And another,
And another,
And another one.
It's like rain coming down.

Quinlan Riley (5)
Fairfields Primary School & Nursery, Flamstead End

The Fizzing Pop!

Pop! Bang!
The firework is exploding,
And is very fast.
Fireworks really banging.
They go out at last.

As colourful as a rainbow,
The gold really glows.
I'm going to pop!
This is really exciting.
You can't be frightened.

Theo Achilleos (9)
Fairfields Primary School & Nursery, Flamstead End

Fireworks Crackle

Fireworks so bright in the sky,
When I watch them my eyes water.
They're as loud as a car,
They're as fast as an aeroplane.

When I hear them,
It gives me a little fright.
They go so high in the air,
They fly so high,
In the night sky.

Ethan Thomas (8)
Fairfields Primary School & Nursery, Flamstead End

Fireworks

Firework colours,
From yellow to blue,
They're all going boom!
Sparkling and glittering.
Boom! Bang! Pop! Pow!
In the sky so high.
Remember, you can find magic
Wherever you look.
Sit back and relax,
All you need is a *boom!*

Ella Carroll (8)
Fairfields Primary School & Nursery, Flamstead End

Fireworks

Flying through the air,
Colours bursting everywhere.
There they go, booming bright,
People having a great fright.
Banging, booming in the air,
People having a big stare.
Sparkles sparkling, popping out fright,
Children's eyes are big and bright.

Millie-Lee Dwyer (8)
Fairfields Primary School & Nursery, Flamstead End

Fireworks, Fireworks!

Fireworks, fireworks,
In the sky,
Say hello to the heavenly sky.

Oh, there not there!
They've vanished,
I don't know,
If next year I can go.

I don't want to wait,
For next year.
Goodbye heaven sky.

Amira Bundu (8)
Fairfields Primary School & Nursery, Flamstead End

Fireworks In The Sky

Fireworks, fireworks,
In the air.
Crackle and pop,
Exploding colours
In the sky.

Unique noises
Everywhere.
Tumbling, flying,
Springing too.

I love fireworks and
I hope you do too!

Fearne James (9)
Fairfields Primary School & Nursery, Flamstead End

Bonfire Night

Fireworks are bright,
Fireworks go *bang* and *pop.*
Fireworks go *zoom,*
Pop! Pop! Pop!
Bang! Bang! Bang!
Zoom! Zoom! Zoom!
The firework goes.

Aksel Acemgil (8)
Fairfields Primary School & Nursery, Flamstead End

Monster Mike

Monster Mike is like a Gruffalo.
Scary Mike is a sleepy and a big monster,
He is the Cookie Monster,
And is way big,
Like a tree.
Monster Mike lives in space,
Along with his friend, Traye.
Monster Mike is watching space TV.
Space Ranger is on the box,
Wearing comfy socks.

Raamin Islam (14)
Piper Hill High School, Newall Green

I Like...

I like doing English,
I like doing maths.
I like doing music,
And swimming in the bath!
I like doing science,
I like doing history.
I like doing computing,
I like sitting well.
I like doing collective worship.

Adam Alferjani (12)
Piper Hill High School, Newall Green

Super School

Our super school
Has amazing teachers.
Teachers are terrific,
Teaching us sensible work,
So we can become geniuses.

Friends are fantastic,
Playing outside together,
So we are friends forever.

Harry Norman Archebald (16)

Piper Hill High School, Newall Green

Super School

I'm going to school,
It's really cool.
In the classroom,
There's no doom and gloom,
Fabulous friends always make amends.
The teachers are terrific,
They make us scientific.

Salim Alqahtani (14)
Piper Hill High School, Newall Green

Cute Cats

Snow is kind,
Helpful, sweet,
Cuddly,
And she loves me
And snuggles on me.
Bella always goes outside,
But she is sweet,
Kind and helpful
And silly.

Tamzin Eyles (14)
Piper Hill High School, Newall Green

About Piper Hill

I love Piper Hill School,
And I enjoy my dinner.
I have friends and teachers,
And I like playing outside,
And I love choice time.

Freya Wilkinson (13)
Piper Hill High School, Newall Green

Unicorn

U nusual

N ice

I ndependent

C ute

O h so lovely

R adiant

N aughty.

Tia Deal (12)
Piper Hill High School, Newall Green

Super School

My friends are silly,
I eat with my friends
In the crazy canteen.
Find a dinner table and
Chat, chat, chat!

Max Gandy (15)
Piper Hill High School, Newall Green

Happy Holiday

On the sandy beach,
The family all meet.
We eat ice cream
And build super sandcastles
With a big bucket.

Bennett Tomy (14)
Piper Hill High School, Newall Green

Perfect Pizza

Dough is delightful,
Terrific tomato tastes magical.
Chunky cheese for me please,
Pepperoni is perfection.

Georgina Johnson (15)
Piper Hill High School, Newall Green

Underwater

Fish, water,
Swim, coral reef,
Fish, tank,
Fish, tunnel,
Sea, fish,
Rocks.

Leo Senobari (12)
Piper Hill High School, Newall Green

Me

My name is Ryan,
I go to school.
I like to play football
And sometimes play pool.

Ryan Johnson (13)
Piper Hill High School, Newall Green

The Big Space Adventure

An alien family up in space searched for buried treasure.

They needed money to buy things for their home.

They searched high and low, there was no time for leisure.

To give them clues of where to go, they sometimes asked a gnome.

On Saturn, the giant Zog made them run away.

On Mars, a tornado stopped them searching more.

On Jupiter, no treasure came, although they dug all day.

On Uranus, they found some shells, not what they were hoping for.

The family went home to Pluto, they felt a little sad.

But a buzzing in the basement made them quite annoyed.

They dug and found gold and jewels, it made them very glad.

They bought lights and carpets and now they're overjoyed!

Rachael Smith (8)
Southborough Primary School, Bromley

Polar Bear In Space

A polar bear woke up in space,
Can you imagine the look upon his face!

Space isn't the polar bear's home,
Although they do quite like to roam.

The cute white bear loved seeing the stars,
As his spaceship sailed past Mars,

Outside the ship, there was no sound,
Inside his fishy dinner floated around!

A dangerous bear, on a dangerous mission,
But his fluffy fur coat was in great condition.

His spaceship suddenly lost control,
It looped and looped and made the bear roll.

He hopes that he will be home soon,
He looks outside and sees the moon.

A smile appears upon his face,
As he finishes his time in space.

Some ice at the North Pole is his landing place.
His trip in space, has been quite outstanding.

Lauren Bewsey (8)
Southborough Primary School, Bromley

My Dream Is A Guitar

I have always wanted
To play the guitar.
One day
I might be a rock star.

The next day,
With a skip and a hop,
I went to a guitar shop.
I went up and down the aisles,
Through the piles
And saw a guitar.
I found the one
And it weighed a ton.

I took it home and started to play,
This was going to be the perfect day.
I wrote a song about going to space,
Then I saw the smile on everyone's face.

I love my guitar,
A dream come true.
Now I'm a rock star,
Maybe you could be too.

Finley Johnston (8)
Southborough Primary School, Bromley

The Wonder Of The Galaxy

A shooting star,
Like white lightning.
A meteor shower rushing down,
Like a rainstorm.
Constellations of stars dazzling,
All of these here,
Before I was born.

Lots of planets in our solar system,
Saturn has a big circle,
Like an onion ring.
Just like a magical kingdom,
The bright sun gives off its bling.

Humans are as tiny as dolls,
But the planets remind me,
Of big, floating emojis.
We explore in the dark,
Like a mole trying to find
The next new discovery.

Emma-Louisa Marie Minas (8)
Southborough Primary School, Bromley

Uni's Day Out

It was Saturday,
The fifth of May,
And Uni was on a day out.
To look for a pom-pom lurking about.
But she found there was no such thing,
At least she met the king.
Mythical Land was great,
Even though she was only eight.
Perfect places everywhere,
Oops! She bumped into a brilliant bear.
Oh, but she really wished to visit Fantasy Land,
It didn't matter if she'd have to chop off her hand.
It was Saturday,
The fifth of May,
And Uni was on a day out.

Rhea Chowdhury (8)
Southborough Primary School, Bromley

The Princess And Her Unicorn

The princess got out of bed
And bumped her head!
She went to her unicorn
And fed it some corn.

Her name is Anna,
Anna's unicorn's name is Hannah.
Anna and Hannah went out,
She took Hannah out and about,
Looking for sprouts,
But Hannah is so lazy.
She sniffed a daisy,
And went all hazy.
At the end of the day,
She had some hay,
'Cause she didn't want to play,
Hannah and Anna went to bed,
And Hannah buried her head.

Jessica Wallace (9)
Southborough Primary School, Bromley

My Best Friend's A Dog

He's fluffy and he's sweet,
He likes cheese and meat.
He loves cuddles,
And is scared of bubbles,
He's protective and fun,
He likes to run and lie in the sun.
Digby hates fireworks,
He's a skeleton on Halloween,
And he likes to play with me.
His ears pop up when I say his name,
And his face is tiny and very cute.
I like to snuggle with him.
He walks in the light,
Not at dark,
Sometimes he's naughty
And likes to bark.

Lacey Hodson (8)
Southborough Primary School, Bromley

The Day I Went To Space

Three, two, one...
We whizzed up,
Past the sun.
We went round and round the stars,
I think we even spotted Mars.

Crash! We landed on the moon,
I hoped I'd get to meet aliens soon.
We were floating in the air,
It was better than a ride at the fair.

Three, two, one...
Space is really super fun.
Now I'm all tucked up back in bed,
Dreaming of more space adventures,
In my head.

Jake Wigley (9)
Southborough Primary School, Bromley

Bob The Alien

Bob likes to eat,
His favourite food is roasted meat.
He likes to run
And he likes to eat his bun.

On hot days he goes for a swim,
Then when he is bored he hides in the bin.
When Bob walks his dog,
He jumps in the muddy bog.

Bob is funny
When he hides in the dunny.
When Bob was little he ate a slug,
Then he got another one and fed it to the pug.

Daniel Cooke (9)
Southborough Primary School, Bromley

The Attack Of Cybermen

C ruel as an executor.

Y elling: "Destroy the Earth!"

B old and fierce like a lion.

E merging out from space.

R aising the level of destruction.

M arching together as an army.

E nding the world as we know it.

N early destroying the Earth!

Benjamin Redgrave (8)

Southborough Primary School, Bromley

Space

S tars sparkling in the night sky.
P lanets positioned around the sun.
A stronauts exploring, discovering new life.
C omets drifting around the galaxy.
E clipse from the moon or sun.

Oliver Jack Dobbs (9)
Southborough Primary School, Bromley

The Rainbow Planet

Once there was a rainbow planet,
It was as round as a football.
It was as colourful as a rainbow,
It was as bright as the sun.
All the other planets were jealous,
Of its colourfulness.

Archie Beaumont (8)
Southborough Primary School, Bromley

Starry Night

The stars are shining,
Shining bright and bold,
Glistening like pure gold.
The stars tonight are brighter than ever,
They seem to be as light as a feather.

Melisa Bafli (9)
Southborough Primary School, Bromley

An Alien Planet

This planet is a
Glorious green colour.
A perfect planet to live on,
Aliens love it here.
A five-star planet,
That's out of this world!

Billy Cranenburgh (8)
Southborough Primary School, Bromley

Aquatic Animals

A beautiful world under the sea, fish can easily eat plastic that subsequently we will digest.

Q uickly our lands and seas are infested with waste.

U nder the skin of a fish, plastic can show.

A fter all the fish do to survive, we kill them with waste.

T o everyone who throws plastic away carelessly, please stop!

I have discomfort when I see waste on the ground,

'C ause I know it will end up in the sea or worse.

A nd even though people say they will stop.

N obody knows how much damage it does.

I t's urgent that we stop throwing plastic away, instead reuse it.

M ore than fifty percent of aquatic animals have decreased.

A round five million tons of plastic is floating in the sea every year.

L ast thing I want is for all aquatic life to die.

S o, will people actually stop throwing plastic carelessly away?

Maia Valentine (11)

Southmuir Primary School, Kirriemuir

Frantic Forest Fires

F irefighters bravely giving their time and lives.

O n the other side of the world, we are donating to help.

R idiculously terrifying sight in the entirety of Australia.

E veryone frantically trying to save their homes and cities.

S ydney's residents are all panicking but some are still giving hope and helping.

T ourists are stranded on beaches and are waiting for the Navy to rescue them.

F orests burning at forty-degree temperatures.

I nternationally famous celebrities are giving all the support they can.

R estrain all your panic and take cover to stay safe.

E ntertain yourself to take your mind off the forest fires.

Daniel Buist (12)
Southmuir Primary School, Kirriemuir

Save The Planet

S top leaving litter on the ground.

A nimals are dying due to climate change.

V aluables in people's homes are being destroyed because of bush fires.

E njoy the Earth whilst it's here.

T hink about the next generation.

H eading towards difficult times.

E arth is changing every day.

P edal to work, do not drive.

L ook to reduce energy consumption at home and at work.

A ll of us need to take part.

N ever give up.

E liminate excessive emissions - electric cars will help.

T rees help to reduce global warming, please do your bit by planting more.

Kieron Robertson (9)

Southmuir Primary School, Kirriemuir

Save Our World

S top using cars as much and walk places.

A nimals are getting hurt because of litter.

V arious forests in Australia are burning.

E very day, the world is changing!

O ur world could be better if we worked together.

U ntil the fire is out in Australia, it will keep burning.

R espect nature and our precious environment.

W herever you are, don't litter.

O cean levels are rising.

R ivers are full of plastic because of littering.

L ittle by little, the Earth is getting warmer.

D ocumentaries have been made about the eight planets.

Caitlyn Fraser (11)

Southmuir Primary School, Kirriemuir

Save The World

S o many animals are dying.

A ustralia's forests are burning down.

V ariety of things can help save the planet.

E mpty trees due to the fires.

T housands of people are risking their lives to put out the fires.

H uge amounts of animals need our help.

E lephants are endangered too.

W ater levels are rising because of the melting ice caps.

O ver time, the animals are dying because of the ice caps melting.

R eady firefighters saving the burning trees.

L ots of trees are getting chopped down.

D eforestation is affecting everyone.

Keirra Brough (11)

Southmuir Primary School, Kirriemuir

Fish In The Sea

Fish in the sea are not like me,
Our world is cleaner than the sea.
Every day there's a new danger,
A piece of plastic from a stranger.

The fish in the sea are dying,
Their numbers aren't multiplying.
The whales are beached more and more,
They come up more than Scottish folklore.

So please help save the fish,
They should be on a dish.
They shouldn't be ill because of us,
We should clean up the plastic, it's not a big fuss!

Healthy fish is good,
It sets you in the right mood.
If you like fish then hear my cry,
There shouldn't be polluted fish in a pie!

Ross Brown (10)
Southmuir Primary School, Kirriemuir

Save The World

S o many animals are dying
A ustralia's forests are burning down
V ariety of things can help save the planet
E mpty trees due to the fires

T housands of people are risking their lives to put out the fires
H uge amount of animals need our help
E lephants are endangered

W ater levels are rising because of the melting ice caps
O ver time, the animals are dying because of the ice caps melting
R eady firefighters to save the burning trees
L ots of trees are getting chopped down
D eforestation is affecting everyone.

Oscar Gray (11)
Southmuir Primary School, Kirriemuir

Planet Earth

P laces on Earth are burning, people are

L osing their homes.

A nimals are losing their homes as well.

N ew families are losing all of their belongings.

E ven land animals are affected by pollution.

T rains, planes, cars and buses are polluting the air.

E very fish you eat has got some plastic in it.

A nimals are dying from all of the plastic.

R educe, reuse, recycle to save Earth.

T he beautiful forests are burning.

H elp save Earth!

Rose Pyott (11)

Southmuir Primary School, Kirriemuir

Friendship

F riends always stick together.

R ecently Liam has moved to Australia.

I remember all the good times we had,

E ven the first time we met.

N ever forget.

D o you still know me? I hope you do.

S oon when I go on holiday I'm coming to see you.

H ope we get a chance to contact each other.

I will never forget about you.

P lease send me a cheerful letter because I'm trying to send a letter to you.

Liam Mcintosh (10)

Southmuir Primary School, Kirriemuir

Climate Change

C hange your ways.

L ess plastic usage.

I ce caps in our polar regions are deteriorating.

M ake a difference.

A large area of forests is ablaze.

T emperature across the globe is rising.

E veryone can help.

C annot give up.

H elp us through these terrible times.

A nimals are suffocating.

N ow is the time to help.

G o and help.

E very little thing helps.

Thomas Watson (11)

Southmuir Primary School, Kirriemuir

Forest Fire

F orests are getting sabotaged.

O ur Earth is getting swept away.

R un away if you want to keep your precious lives.

E vil, burning fires!

S avage fires ruining our lovely green forests.

T urned Australia to ashes.

F ire as hot as lava.

I am praying for rain.

R eeking fires creating hot smoke.

E arth is dying, please help.

Cameron Kelman (11)
Southmuir Primary School, Kirriemuir

Animals

A nimals are losing their homes quickly.

N ature is important to animals.

I ce caps are melting every day.

M ammals in the wild are becoming extinct.

A nimals are in danger from climate change.

L ife is miserable when all the animals are gone.

S omewhere in the world, an animal is losing its pride.

Caela Wallace (11)
Southmuir Primary School, Kirriemuir

Liverpool

L iverpool are the champions.

I am a big fan.

V ictorious in the Champions League.

E nglish team.

R eward is a big, gold trophy.

P osition number one on the table.

O ur biggest rival is Everton.

O ne of the all-time greats, Mo Salah.

L ike to watch a game.

Murray Small (10)

Southmuir Primary School, Kirriemuir

Out Of This World

Haiku poetry

The Earth is dying.
Please help us and save the world,
Animals dying.

Save the turtles now,
Pollution is killing us.
It is all around.

We need your help fast.
Please help us, we need your all,
Help us save the world.

Tia Munro (11)
Southmuir Primary School, Kirriemuir

There's A Monster In The City

There's a monster in the city,
He isn't very small,
He is fifty metres in height,
So he is very tall.

There's a monster in the city,
He is kicking over jars,
He is very furry,
So he is sticking to cars.

There's a monster in the city,
He has a tough tooth, he is chewing on cobbles,
He didn't even have
A microscopic crack in his teeth.
He is near a pond,
He sees a fish blow bubbles.

There's a monster in the city,
He is licking ice from the fridge,
What was he stood on?
Well, it was a bridge!

There's a monster in the city,
He now is leaving.
When he left the city,
People found what they were retrieving.

Oliver Richardson (10)
St Raphael's Catholic Primary School, Stalybridge

Deep Under The Ocean Of Life

Deep under the ocean of life,
The breeze smoothly passes by.
The fish have lots of patterns and colours,
They love to swim through the water.

The bumpy coral is perfect for fish,
It's like coral is their favourite dish.
The moonlight hits the surface of the ocean,
The calm could make you full of emotion.

As the waves hit the shores,
When I say, "Will there be more?"
I watch the trees blowing around,
All you can hear is silence, no sound!

All the stars light up the sky over the water.
It's as calm as the trees, but there will never be terror.
The fish blow bubbles as they go up and down.
There might be treasure like a small crown.

Bethany Gibbons (9)
St Raphael's Catholic Primary School, Stalybridge

Deep Into The Ocean

As the day turns to night,
As the moon takes the role of illuminating the sky,
The tropical fish glide across the salty water,
The seaweed sways side to side,
All of the beautiful colours making the sea
A completely good sight to see.

As the waves, like soldiers, march and march
across the shore,
The sight is not a bore.
As the waves crash against the rocks,
The coral is alive,
It's time for the holidaymakers to arrive.

As the waves crash,
The children laugh,
What can they see?
The dolphins dancing with the waves,
Like ballerinas on a stage,
And I listen as the ocean says,
"It's now time to go to bed."

Katie Wright-Borges (9)
St Raphael's Catholic Primary School, Stalybridge

The Sight Of The Sea

As the day turned to night,
And the moon illuminated the sky,
I stood and gazed at the vast, tranquil ocean
before me.
The dark depths of the ocean whispered to me,
As the waves, like soldiers, approached the shore,
Touching the tip of my toes.

As the tropical fish glided across the grains of the
sand
The flashes of hues left behind a trail.
All these differences brightened up the sea,
Oh, isn't it a wonderful sight to see!

The sound of the waves pushing against the rocks,
Those beautiful colours were hypnotising me,
My footprints got washed away by the shore.
The glimmering gleams of crystals waiting to be
found.

Poppy Evans
St Raphael's Catholic Primary School, Stalybridge

Ocean Life

Where the water reaches the shore,
Whilst the moon takes over the sun,
I am there, watching the sunset at home,
Whilst the sand sinks into my toes.

The moon watches over the sea,
Like a mother watching her child sleep.
The waves are gently hugging the rocks,
Whilst the water steals the sand.

All under the sea
Are beautiful sea creatures,
Living in complete peace.
Now there's a thunderstorm.

All the waves are crashing against the rocks,
Like they are starting WWIII.
The sun is taking over the moon once again,
All the sharks are viciously eating fish.
Oh no! This is a catastrophe.

Harvey Wade (9)
St Raphael's Catholic Primary School, Stalybridge

A Trip To The Ocean

Aboard my ship that only holds two,
It's just enough room for me and you,
Hoist the sail and roll up the anchor.
Our mighty ship, stronger than a tanker.

Ocean so smooth, water so calm,
But just then waters become violent like a bomb.
As waves crash and thrash upon the boat,
Our love fights back, keeping us afloat.

The boat's damaged,
We thank God no one's hurt.

The boat's now gone, but not all is lost,
An item of money with no real cost,
You and I shall not live in vain,
We'll sail upon the ocean of life once again.

Wiktoria Weglarek (10)
St Raphael's Catholic Primary School, Stalybridge

Tomorrow Land

At the end of the day, I wake up and look out my window.
Outside is a totally different land.
I rush outside to see the wonderful world.
Then, my neighbour flies past my face.
I go to the café to get my breakfast and everyone is a robot!

I hop on the train and go flying through the mythical land.
When I arrive at school, there's a massive anti-gravity dome around my school.
At break time, people fly past me in the bendy straw slide like jet planes.
Oh, how wonderful it is to be me!

Hunter Melville-Terry (9)
St Raphael's Catholic Primary School, Stalybridge

The Undersea World

As the brightening day turns into the darkening night,
Under the canyons, a mysterious world comes to life.

I excitedly jump into my submarine,
Whilst the stars, like lanterns, illuminate the sky.

The submarine goes down, down, down,
The sea whispers to me like a human.

I look out the window and see
Sharks swimming, stingrays floating.

Amazing creatures coming to life.
But as the day comes back,
They fall asleep.
Goodnight, sea life.

Sophie Hunt (9)
St Raphael's Catholic Primary School, Stalybridge

Ocean Secrets

As the waves rippled across the sand,
I saw the water spread across the land.

The world just stopped, and I was there,
Standing, breathing in the sea salt air.

All my thoughts left my head,
And I listened as the ocean said,

"These ocean secrets are shared with you,
I've kept them for a long time, and so will you!"

I listened carefully and then left the sea,
These ocean secrets are kept safe with me.

Bethan Hillier (9)
St Raphael's Catholic Primary School, Stalybridge

My Dog

Bone chewer,
Glove pincher,
Kiss giver,
Couch stealer,
Ball taker,
Drooling beast,
Toy thief,
Cat hater,
Tail chaser,
Teddy slayer,
Dog catcher,
Pigeon hunter,
Super swimmer,
Loyal friend,
Food gobbler,
Bush explorer,
Bug eater,
Grass scoffer,
Balloon popper,
Bag destroyer,
Sofa scratcher,

Pillow ripper,
Book shredder,
Shoe breaker,
Last but not least, my dog.

Thomas Rothwell (10)
St Raphael's Catholic Primary School, Stalybridge

My World Of Memories

Somewhere beyond this planet,
Where the stars dance to a gold light,
This gold light controls your eyes,
I begin to see a sight of all sights.

This gold light is my world,
This is where memories grow.
I can remember my life and friends,
I come to this place when I am low.

One day, mean memories crept up,
Bullies made my mind break,
Ruining the memories I make.

Oscar Newton (9)
St Raphael's Catholic Primary School, Stalybridge

Tropical Creatures

As I walk across the sand,
Like bits of sherbert tingling through my toes,
Tropical fish in the sun,
Look like hula girls' skirts.

People watch as the tropical fish
Flick tiny splashes of water
Like sprinkling fairy dust on them.

As the waves approach the shore like soldiers,
The fish prance and dance
As they do, the ground finally twists the buzzer.

Matilda Costello (9)
St Raphael's Catholic Primary School, Stalybridge

The Pacific

Getting to the beach, I never fail,
As I run on the road, not as smooth as tiles.
I reach the beach, the rocks as sharp as nails,
As I look with a gentle smile.

I stare at the illuminated ocean,
No one has seen me, I'm not a failure.
Silence as I look at the water's motion.
I climb into a ship called the Forever Sailor.

Jesse Kyeyune (9)
St Raphael's Catholic Primary School, Stalybridge

Far Into The Ocean

As the blue waves crawl across the sand,
The sun comes and shines on the land.
As the moon illuminates the sun,
My mum says, "Let's go home, son."

As my mum walks home,
I ask, "Can I go on my phone?"
My mum replies, "Not yet,
We are going on a private jet."

Tremaine Norton (10)
St Raphael's Catholic Primary School, Stalybridge

Under The Sea

In the bright, beautiful sea under the bright sun,
Live lots of different coloured fish, swimming back and forth.
Scuba divers explore to find things that haven't been discovered.
Whales as big as houses pass by.
Submarines see deeper waters.
Colourful seashells wash up on the shore.

Riley Norton (9)
St Raphael's Catholic Primary School, Stalybridge

My Little Brother

Munch buncher,
Show-off,
Mess maker,
Game stealer,
Troublemaker,
Bossy boots,
Homework hater,
Terrible terror,
Crybaby,
Money taker,
Animal lover,
Teddy lover,
Best brother,
This is my little brother.

Kian Cassin (10)
St Raphael's Catholic Primary School, Stalybridge

Sir Gryphen

Sir Gryphen,
Winged beast,
Hug giver,
Sky sweeper,
Human lover,
Fish thief,
Feather dropper,
Faithful friend,
Nightmare catcher,
Sleep guardian,
Cloud explorer,
Fear slayer,
The one and only,
Sir Gryphen.

Alice Jones (9)
St Raphael's Catholic Primary School, Stalybridge

My Little Sister

Show-off,
Phone pincher,
Crazy girl,
Crybaby,
Money thief,
Adventure girl,
Bossy boots,
Homework lover,
Cat lover,
Trouble causer,
Mess maker,
Weird sister,
This is my sister.

Thomas Barrientos (9)

St Raphael's Catholic Primary School, Stalybridge

My Fantastic Mum

A kennings poem

Dog walker,
Job doer,
Hard worker,
Sandwich maker,
Make-up lover,
Car driver,
Argument slayer,
Food buyer,
Mess hater,
Animal lover,
Unlike any other,
My mother.

James Bardsley (9)
St Raphael's Catholic Primary School, Stalybridge

My Mum

Cook lover,
Healthy eater,
Peace giver,
Make-up queen,
Argument stopper,
Kiss giver,
Phone hater,
Kindle addict,
Child lover,
That's my super mother!

Katie Cooke (9)
St Raphael's Catholic Primary School, Stalybridge

My Big Brother

A kennings poem

Trouble causer,
Snack eater,
Phone lover,
Seat stealer,
Player outer,
Room stayer,
Argument starter,
Death glarer,
Knuckle cracker,
Anything but my brother.

Frankie Dutton (10)

St Raphael's Catholic Primary School, Stalybridge

Alien Madness

A kennings poem

Troublemaker,
Morning waker,
Tail chaser,
Game player,
Clothes taker,
Prank maker,
Jump scarer,
Noise maker,
Goo thrower,
This is the crazy alien life!

Archie Blay (9)
St Raphael's Catholic Primary School, Stalybridge

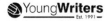

My Alien Creature

A kennings poem

Troublemaker,
Tail chaser,
Three-eyed watcher,
Slime spitter,
Blood pincher,
Hyper hunter,
Kicking killer,
This could only be one thing,
My alien creature!

Belle Forrest (10)

St Raphael's Catholic Primary School, Stalybridge

My Little Sister

A kennings poem

Trouble causer,
Dummy sucker,
Kiss giver,
Nappy leaker,
Milk drinker,
Big hugger,
Noisy giggler,
Toy sharer,
This is my little sister.

Keira Lee (9)
St Raphael's Catholic Primary School, Stalybridge

Dave's Cave

There was an alien named Dave who had a cave,
And its name was Dave Two, he was really brave.
He coloured it pink,
He splattered some ink,
Dave Two always said, "Good morning, Old Dave."

Richard Mankovecky (9)
St Stephen's CE (VA) Primary School, Burnley

Dave The Alien

There was an alien named Dave,
Who had a friend named Maeve,
But he lived on Planet Wizzit,
Too far for Maeve to visit,
Because Maeve lived on Planet Wave.

Joshua Wooding (9)
St Stephen's CE (VA) Primary School, Burnley

There Was An Old Man

There was an old man that lived in a van,
That cooked with his greasy frying pan.
He gazed at the stars,
Thinking about Mars,
And just bought a brand-new pan.

Ophelia Sedgwick (9)
St Stephen's CE (VA) Primary School, Burnley

Dave In A Cave

There was an alien named Dave,
Who lived in a very high cave.
He came out in the light,
But not in the night,
Because he was scared something would wave.

Miley Milliken (10)
St Stephen's CE (VA) Primary School, Burnley

An Alien Named Dave

There was an alien named Dave,
Who wished he had a human slave,
So he hopped on his crane,
And took a trip to Spain,
But the slaves only knew how to shave.

Nicole Lord (9)
St Stephen's CE (VA) Primary School, Burnley

There Was An Old Man With A Plan

There was an old man with a plan,
Who shouted very loud, "I can,
I can go to Mars,
And gaze at the stars,
All I need is a frying pan."

Hollie Murdoch (10) & Amelia Little-Peddar (9)

St Stephen's CE (VA) Primary School, Burnley

Dave

There was an alien named Dave,
And he loved to play with Mave.
He loved to eat fish,
Which he hated on a dish,
But he loved to say hi and wave.

Harry Morton-Hargreaves (9)
St Stephen's CE (VA) Primary School, Burnley

Dave's Cave!

There was an alien named Dave,
Who always surfed the big wave.
He was making a plan,
With his best friend, Stan,
To live in a very rocky cave.

Amelia Parsons (10)
St Stephen's CE (VA) Primary School, Burnley

There Was An Alien Named Dave

There was an alien named Dave,
He lived in a big grey cave.
He had a cute cat,
His name was Mad Bat,
And he lived with his wife named Mave.

Markus Mankovecky (9)
St Stephen's CE (VA) Primary School, Burnley

What Happened To Dave?

There was an alien named Dave,
Who lived in a very fat cave.
He liked to dance,
With his friend, Lance,
But got washed away by a massive wave.

Georgina Pilling (10)
St Stephen's CE (VA) Primary School, Burnley

Brave Dave

There was an alien named Dave,
And Dave the alien was very brave.
He wanted to jump
But he was too plump,
The next day he died in a cave.

Dexter Bennett-Hope (9)
St Stephen's CE (VA) Primary School, Burnley

Dave The Alien

There was an alien named Dave,
He was thinking of having a shave.
It started to tickle,
So he ate a pickle,
While he talked in a cave.

Jovi Fifield (10)
St Stephen's CE (VA) Primary School, Burnley

An Alien Named Dave

There was an alien named Dave,
Who always bathed and bathed.
He got in his tub,
With a rub a dub dub,
And had a very quick shave.

Harun Mitchell-Celep (9)
St Stephen's CE (VA) Primary School, Burnley

Dave And A Black Cat

There was an alien named Dave,
Who liked to go and sunbathe.
He saw a black cat,
And hit it with a bat,
And buried it in a cave.

Lucca Murgatroyd (9)
St Stephen's CE (VA) Primary School, Burnley

Dave Who Went To Mars

There was an alien named Dave,
Who lived in a cave
And went to Mars
To see the stars
And did the great Mexican wave.

Paris Hewitt (10)
St Stephen's CE (VA) Primary School, Burnley

YOUNG WRITERS INFORMATION

We hope you have enjoyed reading this book – and that you will continue to in the coming years.

If you're a young writer who enjoys reading and creative writing, or the parent of an enthusiastic poet or story writer, do visit our website **www.youngwriters.co.uk**. Here you will find free competitions, workshops and games, as well as recommended reads, a poetry glossary and our blog. There's lots to keep budding writers motivated to write!

If you would like to order further copies of this book, or any of our other titles, then please give us a call or order via your online account.

Young Writers
Remus House
Coltsfoot Drive
Peterborough
PE2 9BF
(01733) 890066
info@youngwriters.co.uk

Join in the conversation!
Tips, news, giveaways and much more!

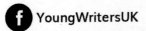 **YoungWritersUK**   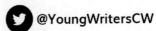 **@YoungWritersCW**